Low-F
Double-Deckers

GAVIN BOOTH

KEY
Books

BRITAIN'S BUSES SERIES, VOLUME 9

Front cover image: Environmental considerations have led to the introduction of low-floor double-deck buses powered by alternatives to diesel fuel. This is one of 17 gas-powered 11.4m (37ft 4in) Scania N280UD with Alexander Dennis Enviro400City 71-seat bodies supplied to Reading Buses, pictured when new in 2018. Distinctive coloured route branding is a feature of the Reading fleet.

Back cover image: London operators have been major customers for low-floor double-deckers. This 2003 London Central Volvo B7TL with Plaxton President 64-seat body is seen crossing Waterloo Bridge in 2008.

Title page image: First's bus companies throughout the UK have received substantial deliveries of Wright-bodied Volvos. Here, crossing Argyle Street in Glasgow in 2005, is a 2004 First Glasgow Volvo B7TL 10.7m (35ft 1in) 74-seater. On the right is another Volvo/Wright combination in the fleet, a 2001 B7L with Eclipse 41-seat body.

Contents page image: When diesel-electric double-deckers first appeared, operators were quick to draw attention to their environmental credentials. Stagecoach initially adopted this green variation of its then-current livery style to highlight its hybrid buses. A 2010 Stagecoach Manchester delivery, featuring a 10.9m (35ft 8in)-long Alexander Dennis Enviro400H 78-seater, prepares to depart for the airport in 2011. Behind it is a Volvo B7TL/Wright from the Finglands fleet.

Published by Key Books
An imprint of Key Publishing Ltd
PO Box 100
Stamford
Lincs PE19 1XQ

www.keypublishing.com

The right of Gavin Booth to be identified as the author of this book has been asserted in accordance with the Copyright, Designs and Patents Act 1988 Sections 77 and 78.

Copyright © Gavin Booth, 2021

ISBN 978 1 802821 29 1

Typeset by SJmagic DESIGN SERVICES, India.

Contents

Introduction

Since 1998, the shape and essence of new double-deck buses for UK customers has changed completely. Where previously prospective passengers had to negotiate entrance steps when boarding a double-deck bus, and there was little or no provision for buggies and wheelchairs, today every bus in normal service is built to a low-floor specification which is fully accessible. The Latin word 'omnibus' means 'for all' – and with the low-floor revolution, the humble bus really has become for all.

First, there were low-floor single-deckers. These had become popular in mainland Europe, and there was forceful lobbying to introduce these into the UK. This happened from 1993, tentatively at first but quickly gaining impetus, with the rising popularity of models like the Dennis Dart.

The next step was inevitably to develop low-floor double-deckers, and these followed from 1998. These were built by manufacturers that already had a foothold in the UK market through sales of step-entrance models, and who realised that demand for low-floor chassis could mirror the swing towards low-floor single-deckers.

The move was hastened by the Disabled Persons Transport Advisory Committee (DPTAC), which introduced regulations that ensured that new buses for local services introduced from 31 December 2000 onwards were suitable for use by passengers with a range of disabilities, including wheelchair users.

This created a rush to get new double-deck models designed and developed, and initially DAF and Dennis introduced low-floor models, with Volvo following close behind after a false start.

This book looks at the way the low-floor double-decker has developed, starting with the earliest models through to the latest hybrid, electric and even hydrogen-powered buses. It is largely chronological, exploring these buses on a model-by-model basis.

Many of the photographs show low-floor double-deckers as they were delivered, with their original owners and in their original livery. Although some have been transferred within the major groups, I have tried to avoid photos of buses that have been sold on to unconnected second and even third owners; that could be a topic for a separate book. Also outside the scope of this book are UK-built or bodied double-deckers for export markets, although a small selection is included to underline the wide range of countries that are coming to UK builders to upgrade their fleets.

I am grateful to the photographers who responded to my call for images to fill in gaps in my own collection. Thanks to Phil Halewood, Roger Hall, Mark Lyons, Keith McGillivray, Robert McGillivray, Richard Walter and Russell Young, and to Alexander Dennis Ltd, who all readily provided images that had eluded me. Their excellent photos are credited throughout the book, and the uncredited photos are mine.

Gavin Booth
Edinburgh

Chapter 1

Lowbridge, Low-Height, Low-Entry or Low-Floor

D ouble-deckers are, by necessity, high. How high, however, has been an issue from the days of the earliest motor buses. It took almost a century, from the introduction of the first motor buses in the UK to the point where a new breed of bus was developed, to provide easy access for all passengers. The low-floor revolution started in the 1990s, but there had been much earlier attempts to make life easier for passengers. For years, though, it seemed that bus builders and bus operators were more concerned about increased seating capacities and better fuel consumption than they were about how easy their buses were to use.

The vast majority of double-deckers built in the first decades of the 20th century were open-topped and used on urban routes. However, they also used high-built chassis so overall height could be a problem for the buses and their unprotected top deck passengers, especially where low railway bridges abounded. Some early attempts to provide covered-top double-deckers produced buses that looked unwieldy and, frankly, were unsafe. Furthermore, passengers had to be fit to climb the steep steps from the pavement to the platform, and brave to climb the narrow staircase to the top deck that was open to the elements.

When bus companies and bus builders recognised that buses could be lower built, in the interests of stability and passenger convenience, the provision of top covers to protect their passengers from the vagaries of the UK weather became easier. This led to game-changing designs like London General's NS type, which was built with covered tops from 1925, and Leyland's Titan of 1927 that popularised the concept of a lowbridge double-decker – one that could cope with low bridges and often low bus garage doors, and still provide comfortable seating for 48 passengers, even if the 24 passengers on the top deck were perched on four-across seats fed from a sunken gangway on the offside. This slightly awkward layout, dubbed lowbridge, was still being incorporated in new buses until 1968, even though more practical solutions had been available for some time.

The lowbridge Leyland Titan had an overall height of just 3.96m (13ft), and the highbridge version that followed was just 4.26m (14ft). These set a pattern, although most lowbridge models that followed were typically around 4.36m (14ft 3in) high and highbridges were 4.42m (14ft 5in) high.

Just four years after the Titan was launched, Gilford, which was enjoying some success in the single-deck coach market, unveiled a remarkable model at the 1931 Commercial Motor Show – a front-wheel drive double-decker with a very low floor height; however, after its debut, no more was heard of it.

Although double-deckers developed greatly between the 1920s and the 1950s, with the introduction of pneumatic tyres, diesel engines and preselective gearboxes, these were practical improvements that made life easier for bus operators and their drivers, if not necessarily for their passengers. Engines were still mounted at the front, with the driver perched alongside and most buses had entrances behind the rear axle, sometimes with doors for out-of-town work. That most iconic of buses, the London Transport Routemaster, was designed in the 1950s as a front-engined, rear entrance bus and the vast majority were built to this layout until production ceased in 1968.

This is not to say that London Transport was behind the times. As the UK's single largest bus operator, designing and specifying buses for London's conditions, it had the resources to experiment, and, in the 1930s, it received batches of buses with side-mounted, underfloor-mounted and rear-mounted engines.

The side-mounted model was the AEC Q, where the engine sat on the offside, behind the driver, and, on some versions, this enabled the front axle to be set back and the passenger entrance situated ahead of this, in line with the driver. Leyland built the underfloor-engined Tiger TF type for London from 1937, although, unlike the underfloor models that followed in the 1950s, there was still a half-cab for the driver and the passenger entrance was still behind the front axle. It was the same for the rear-engined CR type Cub built from 1938 by Leyland, a small 20-seater designed for use in the further reaches of London Transport's Country Area. However, while they were technically advanced, none of these offered low floor levels for passengers.

The two Leyland models might have been the forerunners of large fleets, but as war increasingly became inevitable in the late 1930s, operators and manufacturers were concentrating on more conventional models. So, although only 88 TFs and 49 CRs were built, London Transport was gaining experience that would be reflected in some of its post-war designs.

Leyland was experimenting with new concepts. In 1935, it introduced the Leyland-GEC Low-Floor Trolley Bus, a remarkable 9.14m (30ft)-long three-axle double-deck trolleybus with a flat lower deck floor and an entrance ahead of the rear axle with another behind the rear axles. At just 4.11m (13ft 5in) high, it anticipated designs that would become familiar 25 years later. It was demonstrated to a number of trolleybus operators but may just have been too far ahead of its time to go into production.

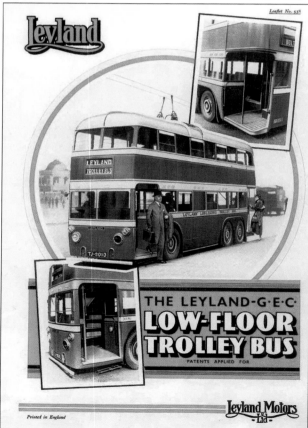

Another advanced three-axle bus was the Leyland Panda, but its twin steering axles were at the front, and its passenger door between the front and rear axles. It had an underfloor-mounted engine, and the chassis was delivered to the Scottish operator, W Alexander, which built a 45-seat body on it.

In 1936, Leyland built an experimental single-decker with its petrol engine mounted transversely at the rear – a foretaste of the layout that would become standard on UK-built double-deckers from the 1960s to the present day. There is a suggestion that this bus, which never ran in passenger service, was produced in the knowledge that rear-engined buses were

The cover of a manufacturer's brochure for the 1935 Leyland-GEC Low-Floor Trolley Bus demonstrates forward thinking that, in this case, came to nothing.

already in production in the United States, and Leyland was also aware that Midland Red had built rear-engined prototype single-deckers in 1935–36.

Midland Red had the largest UK bus fleet outside London and designed and built its own buses in Birmingham. Its rear-engined buses were not entirely satisfactory in this form, and they were converted with mid-mounted underfloor engines to become the predecessors of a large fleet; the first production examples entered service in 1946, while UK manufacturers were still struggling to return to normal after six years of concentrating on military vehicles.

The idea of a flat 'pancake' engine, which could be mounted under the floor of single-deckers, was not new. American builders had been producing these since the early 1930s because it released the entire interior of the bodywork behind the driver and the door for seated passengers. The idea caught on slowly in the UK in the late 1940s, as the main manufacturers realised that this was the future. When 9.14m (30ft)-long single-deckers were legalised in 1950, the floodgates opened; very quickly, most operators adopted underfloor-engined single-deckers with seats for up to 45 passengers, replacing front-engined models that typically had seats for only 35.

While underfloor-engined single-deckers were useful crowd-movers, the engine position meant there was a high-floor line and passengers usually had to negotiate a narrow entrance with three or four steep steps. These were not buses suited to people with disabilities or parents with prams or buggies but were eagerly adopted by bus company traffic departments. Midland Red produced two underfloor-engined double-deckers in 1960–61, but they never caught on – although, more than 20 years later, Volvo and Leyland produced underfloor-engined double-deck chassis based on existing single-deck models. These enjoyed some success, even at a time when there was increasing pressure on bus companies to offer buses that were accessible to passengers who needed entrances that were wider and lower.

Mainstream double-deckers remained resolutely front-engined until the late 1950s. Most urban buses had highbridge (by this time referred to as 'normal-height') bodies, and, as vehicle dimensions were relaxed, typical examples had seats for 56, later increasing to 66, and then to 9.14m (30ft) in length with seats for up to 75 passengers. The majority had open rear entrances under the control of a conductor, but in the late 1950s, forward entrances just behind the front axle became popular. Lowbridge bodies, with those awkward side gangways on the upper deck, continued to be popular with some operators right up until 1968, by which time they were usually 9.14m (30ft)-long buses with seats for up to 67 passengers.

To achieve lower overall heights on traditional front-engined double-deckers, the lowbridge layout was traditionally adopted, with this layout for the upper deck – a sunken offside gangway and a step up to four-across seating. Although the Bristol Lodekka was available to state-owned companies and AEC, Albion and Dennis offered similar layouts with normal seating on both decks, the lowbridge layout was still chosen by some operators into the late 1960s.

Bristol and Eastern Coach Works (ECW) were state-owned bus builders supplying state-owned fleets, which, in the 1950s, were the Tilling and Scottish groups and London Transport. They built the great majority of new buses for the Tilling companies, as well as a proportion of new buses for the Scottish companies, while London Transport went its own way and only bought small batches of ECW bodies.

In 1949, Bristol and ECW unveiled a revolutionary new design of double-decker, the Lodekka, which used a dropped-centre rear axle to enable a flat floor into the lower deck from the rear platform and normal seating on both decks within the overall 'lowbridge' height of 4.36m (14ft 3in). The Lodekka in 60-seat, and later 76–78-seat forms, was in production until 1968, and, although it spawned generally available imitators from AEC and Leyland, and a version built under licence by Dennis, none of the others came anywhere near to equalling the Lodekka's success.

So, there were lowbridge and now low-height double-deckers, but none met the requirements for total accessibility for passengers.

Leyland's rear-engined Atlantean chassis, introduced in 1958, broke the mould and indicated the way double-deck buses would be for the next six decades. With a lower entrance ahead of the front axle and seats for up to 78 passengers, it was an ideal urban bus. If operators wanted a lower overall height, then Leyland and Metro-Cammell offered a version with a side gangway and higher-mounted seats towards the rear of the upper deck, but this was far from popular. So, when Daimler introduced its Fleetline model, enabling normal seating on both decks within the 'lowbridge' height, several operators changed allegiance. Some Atlantean and Fleetline deliveries had no steps to the lower saloon and a ramped floor; others provided a single shallow step.

Meanwhile, single-deckers were moving away from the underfloor-engined layout and towards rear-engined models with a flat engine mounted under the floor at the rear of the saloon. While these were not yet fully accessible buses, they were much easier for passengers to use, and there was increasing attention paid to passenger requirements. Floor heights could be low with a rear engine, doorways wider and entrance steps fewer and shallower.

Jump forward to the 1970s, and a new breed of bus was appearing in mainland Europe. Double-deck buses were relatively rare in Europe; a few major cities, including Berlin, Lisbon and Vienna, had been enthusiastic double-deck customers, but long single-deckers were the buses of choice in most other places. One increasingly important issue was the continental height limit of 4m (13ft 1in), and this particularly affected double-deck coaches, which had become increasingly popular for longer-distance express services. Builders like Neoplan produced their impressive Skyliner models to the 4m height by designing an underframe with a flat lower saloon floor. It had also built easy-access airside buses for European airports. With this knowledge, Neoplan turned to its single-deck bus range and responded to a call that was becoming louder – for fully accessible service buses.

Neoplan built the first low-floor buses in Germany in 1977, and in 1986, wheelchair access with ramps followed. In the Netherlands, The Hague bought low-floor Neoplans in 1991, and low-floor buses quickly became the vehicles of choice across much of Europe. In the UK, operators were watching these developments with interest, and in 1992, four low-floor buses were brought to Liverpool from mainland Europe for Merseytravel to inspect. These were a Den Oudsten Alliance City, a MAN/Berkhof, a Neoplan N4014 and a Van Hool A300.

These gave UK operators an opportunity to inspect the new breed of low-floor buses first hand. At the same time, London Buses had ordered 68 low-floor single-deckers – 38 on the new Dennis Lance SLF chassis and 30 on the Scania N113, all with Wright bodies. These entered service in 1994, following single low-floor buses delivered to Merseytravel (Neoplan) and Tayside (Scania).

However, heavyweight – and expensive – low-floor single-deckers were not what every UK bus company wanted, and Dennis saw the opportunity to produce a low-floor version of its successful

Neoplan was a pioneer of low-floor single-deck buses, and early deliveries went to HTM in The Hague in the Netherlands. The low side window line is a result of the low floor line.

Dart midibus chassis, which then went on to outsell all the others. Dennis had been a low volume bus chassis builder for many years but with the Dart and, as we shall see, the Trident double-decker, it was propelled into the first division.

With a few notable exceptions where double-deckers are used, bus companies in mainland Europe use articulated buses to move large numbers of passengers. Articulated single-deckers have been tried in the UK with mixed success, notably in London and with FirstGroup companies, but rigid single-deckers and double-deckers seem to suit bus operators and, importantly, their customers.

By the late 1990s, most UK bus operators were buying low-floor single-deckers and attention was turning to the possibilities of double-deck equivalents. Even the term 'low-floor' can be misleading. Strictly speaking, a low-floor bus offers a low floor throughout, while most 'low-floor' buses built for use in the UK are strictly 'low-entry', with a floor that is flat for much of the interior but has steps towards the rear to accommodate mechanical components. However, for the purposes of this book, the term low-floor covers both low-entry and low-floor models.

At the Coach & Bus show in 1995, DAF exhibited a low-floor double-deck chassis, the DB250LF, which combined the low front section from its SB220LF single-deck model with the drivetrain of its existing DB250 step-entrance double-decker. This gave DAF a head-start in the race to get low-floor double-deckers into production.

Volvo was next into the fray, but it misjudged what UK operators would require. It exhibited a bus with the new Plaxton President body at the 1997 Coach & Bus show, but with its engine mounted in the rear nearside corner and a long rear overhang, it was not what the UK market wanted, so Volvo went back to the drawing board to come up with the transverse-engined B7TL model in 1999. This meant that Volvo missed out on early orders to DAF and to Dennis, which had moved decisively into the big league with its Dart midibus and now offered its Trident low-floor double-decker. Even before it was launched, nearly 300 orders had been placed and the British double-deck bus was about to undergo a major change.

The low-height double-deck pioneer was the Bristol Lodekka, with a flat lower deck floor, but no access for prams or wheelchairs. This is a 1968 Eastern Counties 70-seat FLF6G, photographed in Cambridge.

In 1958, the Leyland Atlantean represented the first step towards practical low-floor double-deckers, with its rear-mounted engine and entrance ahead of the front axle. The upper deck layout shows how Leyland and Metro-Cammell Weymann (MCW) attempted to provide a low-height double-decker with a raised area towards the rear. Next, Daimler Fleetline came along with a chassis for a proper low-height bus, but there would be no easy access for people with disabilities or wheelchair users for another 40 years.

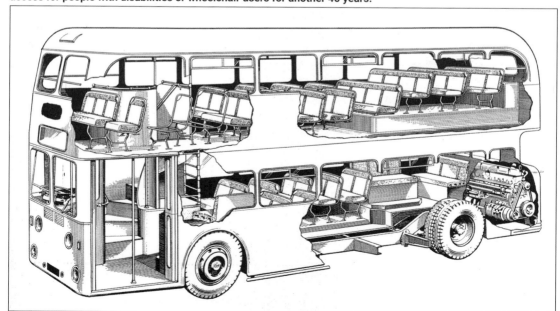

Above: Low-floor buses are most effective when passengers can step from the kerb straight onto the platform, unlike this pioneering Centrewest Dennis Lance SLF with Wright body, which is seen loading at the Uxbridge terminus of the 222 route in 1994.

Right: For many, the first sight of a practical low-floor double-decker was this three-axle Dennis Trident with ALX500 body for the KMB Group in Hong Kong. Bodied in Falkirk, it was shown to Lothian Region Transport managers in January 1998, before export to Hong Kong.

This was the low-floor double-decker shown to potential customers in 1998, proclaiming itself to be a Plaxton President, with no obvious reference to Volvo, which had provided the B7L chassis, based on an existing single-deck model. Operators were unhappy with the engine layout and position – in the nearside rear corner – as well as the long rear overhang, prompting Volvo to go back to the drawing board to conceive the hugely successful B7TL model.

Low-floor single-deckers had been familiar in the UK since the mid-1990s, and the Dennis Dart-Plaxton Pointer combination was the most popular. This 1998 example is in service with First Eastern Counties at Bury St Edmunds station in 2011.

In London, the role of the double-decker as an efficient crowd-mover was called into question by a decision to place nearly 400 low-floor articulated buses in service; the chosen buses were Mercedes-Benz Citaro O530Gs, with three-door bodies and space for 140 passengers, just 49 of them seated. Arriva and Go-Ahead examples are seen together at Victoria in 2009; the 38 and 73 had previously been double-deck routes. The London artics were considered dangerous and consequently lasted fewer than ten years in London service.

Chapter 2

The Suppliers

Until the very end of the 1960s, if UK operators wanted new double-deckers, they would inevitably be built in Britain. During the 1960s, Leyland had absorbed all its one-time competitors – AEC, Bristol, Daimler and Guy – and was developing standard models to sell to any operator needing double-deckers. Some operators expressed their dissatisfaction with this monopoly by encouraging other manufacturers to develop competing double-deck models. The two Swedish giants, Scania and Volvo, gained a foothold in the mid-1970s with their Metropolitan and Ailsa models, while UK-based Dennis burst back into the model lists in 1977 with the Dominator. These models enjoyed some success, but real competition arrived when Metro-Cammell Weymann (MCW), which had formerly concentrated on building bodies on other chassis, introduced its integral Metrobus model and won substantial orders from London and from the Passenger Transport Executive fleets. Leyland and MCW battled it out until 1988, when Leyland Bus sold to Volvo Bus, which gave Volvo an entry into the mainstream double-deck market with an upgraded version of Leyland's bestselling Olympian chassis. The demise of Leyland could have been a sales opportunity for MCW, but its owners, the Laird Group, decided to call it a day in 1989 and sold its road transport interests.

The MCW closure opened doors for Netherlands-based DAF Bus, which bought the rights to the design of the MCW Metrobus chassis, and used elements in its new step-entrance DB250 chassis in 1991. This gave DAF a head-start when low-floor double-deckers were first being considered, as it took the front end from its existing SB220 low-floor single-decker and married it with the rear end of the DB250 to create the DB250LF, first shown in chassis form at the 1995 Commercial Show – the first public indication of the new breed of buses that would follow. In 1998, the first low-floor double-deckers supplied to UK operators were on DAF chassis, with Optare bodywork as the Spectra, and with Alexander ALX400 bodies for Arriva London.

Dennis followed in 1998, with its low-floor Trident double-decker. The company had built double-deck chassis for many years, though typically in low volumes and to a select group of customers. Its step-entrance Dominator had broadened its customer base, but it was propelled into the top rank of UK bus builders with its bestselling Dart midibus chassis, first in step-entrance form and, from 1995, in SLF low-floor form. The low-floor double-deck Dennis Trident was initially conceived in three-axle form for customers in the Far East and was adapted for domestic use as a two-axle chassis, quickly winning business from a wide range of operators.

Volvo, which had dominated the UK step-entrance double-deck market was slower off the mark. It had developed a low-floor double-deck chassis based on its B7 European single-deck model, and a prototype received a new-style body from Plaxton, the President. This bus appeared at the 1997 Commercial Show, but, while Plaxton's contribution was well received, Volvo was uncharacteristically unforthcoming about the chassis underneath. Operators were more vocal – criticising the long rear overhang and the engine compartment in the rear nearside corner. The prototype visited various potential customers – it usually arrived on the back of a low-loader – but this did not generate any more enthusiasm.

Volvo went back to the drawing board and came up with a much more competitive chassis – the B7TL and its stablemate, the B7L. The first examples appeared in service in 1999, and substantial orders quickly followed.

The OmniCity was a complete Polish-built low-floor double-deck model produced by Scania. An OmniCity of Solent Blue Line in Southampton is seen in 2009, wearing the Uni-link livery on a service for the University of Southampton. It is a dual-door 68-seater. (Mark Lyons)

Next up was Scania, which had supplied step-entrance double-deck chassis to the UK market between 1980 and 2000 and entered the low-floor fray in 2003 with the OmniDekka, a bus developed jointly with the bodybuilder East Lancs, and marketed as a Scania product. Scania added the OmniCity in 2005, an all-Scania product built in Poland, and, in 2006, introduced the N2xxUD series of chassis, which would be bodied by Alexander and East Lancs/Optare.

In 2005, Alexander Dennis Ltd (ADL), as it had become following the rescue of the Alexander and Dennis companies after the collapse of the Mayflower Group, upgraded its double-deck offering, which was launched as the Enviro400, in tune with its existing single-deck Enviro200 and Enviro300 models. This introduced a more rounded appearance, with the front upper deck window merging in with the roof. This became ADL's standard offering, completed at Falkirk on its own Guildford-built Dennis chassis for the next nine years.

The German builder, MAN (Maschinenfabrik Augsburg-Nürnberg), which had been hovering at the edges of the UK coach and bus market, unveiled the ND243 model at the 2006 Commercial Motor Show. This was a 4m (13ft 1in)-high, 11.2m (36ft 7in)-long double-decker with East Lancs bodywork, and, while one bus was built and demonstrated to potential customers, it remained unique.

Volvo upgraded its low-floor double-deck offering in 2006–07 to meet imminent Euro V emissions regulations. The B9TL and B9L replaced the popular B7TL and B7L models, and, in 2009, Volvo anticipated future emissions controls with its hybrid diesel-electric B5LH. Other manufacturers had introduced hybrid double-deck models aimed largely at the London market – Wright in 2007 and ADL in 2008.

A high-profile model designed for London operations was the New Routemaster, which reimagined double-deck requirements, at least for Transport for London area. Following design competitions,

Wright was entrusted with the production of 1,000 New Routemasters between 2012 and 2018, all but one 11.3m (37ft 1in)-long with front, centre and rear doors. As originally conceived, passengers could board or alight using any of the three doors, with the supervised open rear platform available for passengers to hop on and off, but, like the rest of the fleet, the doors on the New Routemasters were all controlled by the driver.

The Volvo B5TL replaced the successful B9TL model in 2013–14, and this in turn was joined by the three-axle B8L in 2017–18.

Wright was moving to the construction of complete buses with a small batch of experimental hybrid double-deckers, then the New Routemaster and, in between, had built the 2DL model around VDL running units in 2009–13, mainly for Arriva London. It also produced the integral StreetDeck model from 2014.

Alexander Dennis again upgraded its double-deck design in 2014 with the Major Model Change (MMC) design, which freshened up the Enviro400 range and spawned the Enviro400 City, designed principally for the London market, which had more than a flavour of the New Routemaster about it.

Optare, which had worked with DAF on the low-floor Spectra, had been concentrating on its single-deck range, but, in 2014, it unveiled its Metrodecker, first as a diesel version and then, from 2015, as a full electric bus.

BCI (Bus & Coach International), an Australian business manufacturing buses in China, entered the UK double-deck market in 2016 with its Enterprise model, in two-axle and three-axle form.

It was a boom time for bodybuilders too. The three longest established businesses, Alexander, East Lancs and Northern Counties, had been well placed to body the new breed of low-floor chassis when they first appeared in the late 1990s. Alexander, based in Falkirk, had the greatest capacity, while East Lancs at Blackburn was reinventing itself and shaking off its reputation as a supplier of solid but visually unexciting bodies aimed at the municipal market. Northern Counties, on the other hand, busy in the municipal and PTE markets, had been bought by Plaxton, and, although it continued to produce double-deck bodies at Wigan until 2005, its low-floor offering, the President, was badged as a Plaxton product.

As had happened in the UK bus chassis market, the demise of Leyland saw the disappearance of trusted bodybuilders like Eastern Coach Works, Park Royal and Roe, and there was a complex series of acquisitions that shook up the remaining players. There had been one new builder of double-deckers, Leeds-based Optare, rescued from the ashes of the Roe business, and over the years it was variously owned by the United Bus group, by its management, by North American Bus Industries, the Darwen Group and Ashok Leyland. Although Optare has specialised in stylish single-deckers, its Spectra and Metrodecker models have won useful orders.

However, it was not plain sailing for any of the UK double-deck bodybuilders. In 2001, TransBus International was created when the Mayflower Corporation, which had bought the Alexander business in 1995 and Dennis in 1998, merged with Henlys, which owned Plaxton. By 2004, Mayflower was in administration and what became Alexander Dennis was bought by Scottish investors, while Plaxton was the subject of a management buyout; in 2007, ADL bought Plaxton. In 2019, ADL was sold to the Canadian NFI Group.

While these developments significantly altered the shape and capacity of the bodybuilding industry, new entrants saw an opportunity. Wright, a family firm based in Ballymena, Northern Ireland, had been building single-deck bus and coach bodies mainly for local markets for more than 30 years, but, after some success in the British market in the early 1990s with a range of stylish single-deckers, it dipped a toe in the double-deck market with its distinctive Eclipse Gemini range.

With demand for double-deckers at a peak, particularly buses for London service, the Eclipse Gemini became a popular choice mainly on Volvo, but also on DAF/VDL chassis. Alexander and

Arriva Merseyside has bought Alexander Dennis Enviro400MMCs like this 79-seat 2017 example in Queen Square, Liverpool, in 2018. Deliveries to many fleets in recent years offer free WiFi and USB charging for their passengers. (Russell Young)

Plaxton initially built on Dennis, DAF and Volvo chassis, and Alexander Dennis concentrated on building complete buses on Dennis chassis, and bodies on Scania and a few Volvo chassis. The Dennis Trident was available for bodying by other builders, but East Lancs bodies could be found on Dennis, DAF, Scania and Volvo chassis.

DAF Bus was renamed VDL Bus in 2003 as part of the VDL Groep, which had brought together other Dutch-based bus and coach builders.

Scania worked with East Lancs to produce the OmniDekka, and, in 2005, it launched the OmniCity with its own Polish-built bodywork. More recently, Egyptian-built MCV bodies have appeared on Volvo chassis and complete Chinese-built BCI buses have been bought by UK operators. Another significant Chinese business supplying the UK market is BYD, which provides the chassis for Alexander Dennis fully electric double-deckers.

Today, operators have the choice of EuroVI diesel, hybrid diesel-electric, gas, battery electric and hydrogen models.

Chapter 3
The Customers

By the time low-floor double-deckers came on stream in the UK, the shape of the UK bus industry had largely settled after the frantic sales and acquisitions in the post-deregulation and post-privatisation 1980s and 1990s. The major groups – Arriva, FirstGroup, Go-Ahead, National Express and Stagecoach – served a significant proportion of Britain's bus passengers, along with smaller groups like Blazefield, EYMS, MTL and (Yorkshire) Traction, and the largest of the diminishing band of local authority operators like Cardiff, Lothian, Nottingham, and Reading. In Northern Ireland, Translink's Citybus and Ulsterbus operations were the main potential customers for double-deckers. The groups that had gained dominance in Britain had grown out of the privatisation of the National Bus Company, Scottish Bus Group and the Passenger Transport Executives, and by subsequent acquisitions.

For the bus manufacturers, the most important double-deck market of all was London. Once dominated by the giant enterprise that was London Transport, by the end of the 1990s, the city was served by a range of operators, large and small, that had won tenders to operate London routes. The major London operators had been largely formed by acquisition of London Buses subsidiaries. In 1999, the main players were Arriva, FirstGroup, Go-Ahead, London United, Metroline and Stagecoach, and more than 20 years on, most of these are still dominant in London, even if corporate ownership has changed over the years.

In 2000, Transport for London (TfL) was set up and moved to unify the image of London buses with a generally red scheme and became more prescriptive in the specification of the buses when it was awarding new franchises.

London has always been the best market for new buses in the UK, and although the proportion of single-deckers specified for London routes has increased over the years, double-deckers have been preferred as crowd-movers for high-frequency routes – except for a couple of lapses when London flirted with high-capacity single-deckers in the 1960s, and when 390 articulated single-deckers were introduced from 2002, mainly as an alternative to double-deckers, but which had all been withdrawn from London service by 2011.

By the end of 1999, London operators already had more than 1,000 low-floor single-deckers in service, including more than 800 Dennis Darts, and the manufacturers saw London orders as prime targets. As a result, there was a rush to get low-floor double-deckers into production, and these were often designed from the outset to meet London specifications. The sheer numbers of these buses that were required often meant that operators had to dual source their orders in the rush to update their fleets and meet the dates when new tenders started.

DAF and Dennis initially had the market to themselves when the first orders came in, to be joined belatedly by Volvo. With three major builders offering low-floor chassis, some operators shopped around while others quickly concentrated on just one supplier, if they could.

There was an initial rush to order the two readily available types – the DAF DB250LF and the Dennis Trident. However, although Volvo came late to the party with its B7TL model, it quickly made up for lost time. Although the largest orders for low-floor double-deckers were placed by London operators and the big groups, there were significant local authority customers and forward-looking independents.

The well-known Lincolnshire independent operator, Delaine of Bourne, was an enthusiastic customer for Volvo double-deckers. This is a 2012-delivered B9TL with 75-seat Wright Gemini 2 body – note the DBL registration mark, which appears on many of Delaine's buses; it is in Northborough in 2016. (Russell Young)

Compared with the step-entrance double-deckers that had preceded them, early London low-floor double-deckers offered remarkably few seats for passengers – sometimes even fewer than the 64 seats offered in a much shorter standard-length Routemaster, placed in service 40 years earlier. The physical layout of a low-floor double-decker meant that wheelarch intrusion, the requirement for wheelchair spaces and the centre door restricted the number of seats that could be fitted. Some overcame this with longer buses than had previously been thought necessary.

Outside London, where single-door double-deckers tended to be specified, local authority fleets like Lothian and Nottingham went for extra-long buses that could accommodate up to 90 seated passengers. Generally, double-deckers became longer to offer more space for seated passengers and grew from a typical length of just under 10m (32ft 8in) up to 12m (39ft 4in) in some cases.

As orders for low-floor double-deckers increased, many customers dual-sourced orders to ensure delivery, particularly where buses were needed to fulfil London contracts. Other manufacturers developed new models to meet the demand, so Scania enjoyed periods of sales success and new entrants dipped a toe in the UK double-deck market.

Stagecoach built up a substantial fleet of Dennis Tridents with Alexander bodies in the 2000s and became an important customer for ADL and Scania double-deck products; FirstBus bought a range of double-deck types but formed a close relationship with the Volvo/Wright combination; Arriva, with a sister company importing DAF chassis, became the major customer for the DAF DB250LF, and National Express and Go-Ahead accumulated a range of different types.

With more low-floor double-deck chassis on the market, most of the big groups sampled Scania models and some bought Wright models, notably the VDL-based Gemini 2DL and the StreetDeck; the main London companies also operated the 1,000 New Routemasters that were bought by Transport for London.

More than 20 years after the first low-floor double-deckers took to the road in the UK, the structure of the operating industry is still much the same. The large groups – Arriva, First, Go-Ahead, National Express and Stagecoach – still have the greatest buying power, and there are smaller groups that have made their presence felt around the country, including Rotala, Transdev, Wellglade and West Coast. In London, the dominant players are Abellio (owned by the Dutch national rail operator, Nederlandse Spoorwegen), Arriva (owned by the German national rail operator, Deutsche Bahn), Metroline (owned by Comfort DelGro of Singapore), London United (owned by RATP-DEV of Paris) and Go-Ahead and Stagecoach (both UK-owned).

The local authority sector, once a significant customer for double-deckers, has reduced greatly over the past half-century; from a peak of around 100 municipalities running their own buses, just eight remain and the largest of these – Blackpool, Cardiff, Lothian, Nottingham and Reading – continue to invest in new double-deckers.

Chapter 4

DAF/VDL DB250LF

DAF began in 1928 in Eindhoven, in the Netherlands, first building trucks, then buses and then private cars. DAF dipped a toe in the UK bus and coach market with coach chassis in 1975 and single-deck bus chassis from 1988. In 1989, it combined with Dutch coachbuilder Bova to form United Bus, with other builders joining, notably Leeds-based Optare. United Bus collapsed in 1993 and DAF Bus joined the VDL Groep, which included other coachbuilders; in 2003, the name VDL Bus replaced DAF Bus.

DAF's move into the UK double-deck market followed the closure of MCW in 1989, when DAF bought the rights to MCW's Metrobus chassis. The Metrobus rear axle, suspension and transversely mounted engine were incorporated into DAF's new step-entrance DB250 model. The low-floor version was announced in 1997 and, working with Optare, ensured that DAF was first to get this new breed of double-deck into passenger-carrying service in the UK in February 1998.

DAF's DB250LF was the first low-floor double-decker that UK operators could buy, so it attracted a rush of early orders and continued to be bought in substantial numbers by Arriva London and other Arriva fleets in England and Wales. Arriva's sister company, Arriva Bus & Coach, was the UK's DAF Bus importer, so the Arriva operations in London and in other parts of the country became the most enthusiastic customers. The DB250LF was bodied by Alexander, East Lancs, Optare and Plaxton, and Wright.

Photographed in Bristol in 2000, Abus of Bristol's R222 AJP, a 1998 DAF DB250LF with Optare Spectra 81-seat bodywork, declares itself to be 'Britain's first low floor fully *accessible* [sic] double deck bus'.

Above: Another of the handful of R-registered low-floor double-deckers was Arriva London's first DB250LF, with 10.6m (34ft 8in) Alexander 62-seat ALX400 body, a style that would quickly become familiar over the next few years. In 1998, this was the first low-floor double-decker to operate in London, and it is seen here at Turnpike Lane in 2000. (Roger Hall)

Left: Travel West Midlands (TWM) was an early customer for the DB250LF/ Optare Spectra combination, buying 22 in 1998–99. The first carries the appropriate R1 NEG registration – TWM was part of the National Express Group. It is seen at Birmingham's Moseley Road station in 1999. (Roger Hall)

UK North was a short-lived Manchester-area independent operator, and it bought four early examples of the DB250LF with 69-seat Alexander ALX400 bodywork in 1999.

Above: Wilts & Dorset bought 32 Optare Spectra 78-seat DB250LFs between 1998 and 2003. This 2000 78-seat example is in Christchurch. (Mark Lyons)

Right: Reading Buses was another early customer for the DB250LF/ Optare Spectra combination. This 2002 74-seat example, seen in central Reading in 2004, carries LowRider branding. (Mark Lyons)

Arriva Yorkshire operated step-entrance and low-floor DAF/ Spectras, buying 24 DB250LF 74-seaters in 2002. This one is in City Square, Leeds, in 2011, passing one of the innovative articulated Wright StreetCars from First's Leeds fleet.

Ipswich Buses is one of the dwindling band of local authority-owned bus fleets in Britain. This is a 2003 DB250 with East Lancs Myllennium Lowlander 72-seat body, one of six bought in 2002–04. It is seen here in 2007. (Mark Lyons)

The DB250LF chassis also sold to independent operators. This VDL-badged example with East Lancs Lowlander bodywork was new to TM Travel of Chesterfield in 2004. Blackburn-based East Lancs produced similar bodies on a range of chassis, with different body names appropriate to the make of chassis; this body on the Dutch-built DAF chassis was the Lowlander, and, in this case, specifically a Myllennium Lowlander with the squarer front end.

Konectbus of Dereham bought four Wright Pulsar Gemini-bodied 65-seat VDL DB250LFs in 2005. This one is photographed when new at the Thickthorn Park & Ride site in Norwich on a P&R service. (Mark Lyons)

Wrights of Ballymena built its first double-deck bodies in 2001, and these quickly became a familiar sight throughout the UK on DAF and Volvo chassis. The distinctive shape of the Wright Pulsar Gemini body is evident in this 2009 view of a 2005 Arriva London 65-seat example at Islington Green. The distinctive 'cow's horn' above the driver's cab identified Arriva's London fleet in the days before Transport for London's all-red policy came in.

Arriva Midlands received 32 of these Wright Pulsar Gemini-bodied DB250s in 2006, as seen here in Wigston in 2006, carrying LocalLinx's *turn up & go!* branding. (Mark Lyons)

Wright developed this lower-height version of the Pulsar Gemini for Arriva fleets, omitting the distinctive rounded top of the normal-height version. Here is an Arriva Merseyside 71-seat DB300 example, new in 2011, against the impressive backdrop of Liverpool's St George's Hall in 2012.

Chapter 5

Dennis Trident

D ennis is the great survivor among UK bus builders, tracing its beginnings back to 1895. Over the years, it developed a range of bus chassis, which have been sold to a select group of customers. It was only in the 1980s and 1990s that it moved into the big league with a range of innovative single-deck designs, notably the iconic Dart.

Ownership of Dennis changed frequently during the 30 years from 1977 – being purchased by Hestair, Trinity and Mayflower/TransBus – but following problems at Mayflower, a consortium bought TransBus Alexander and Dennis and renamed the business Alexander Dennis Ltd. In 2019, ADL was sold to Canadian-based New Flyer Industries (NFI).

The first Dennis Tridents were three-axle double-deckers for Hong Kong, but, following the company's success with the Dart, it quickly developed a two-axle version for the UK market, and this first appeared in service in 1999 and early examples joined Stagecoach's London fleet, Brighton & Hove, Capital Citybus, Lothian, Metroline, Nottingham and Oxford. Bodywork was mainly the Alexander ALX400, but the Trident was also bodied by East Lancs, Optare and Plaxton.

The Stagecoach London fleets were enthusiastic early customers for the Dennis Trident with Alexander ALX400 bodywork. Stagecoach bought its first in January 1999 and went on to build up a fleet of some 900 similar buses for its London operations. This one stands out against a threatening sky in Hackney in 2000.

Above: The Bournemouth local authority operator, trading as Yellow Buses, bought a batch of nine early Tridents with East Lancs Lolyne 84-seat bodies in 1999 – note the 'Super Low Floor' legend above the destination display in this 2004 image. (Mark Lyons)

Left: Two 1999 Tridents with 9.9m (32ft 5in) Plaxton President bodies from First's Capital fleet lay over at the Oxford Circus terminus of London's 25 route. Before the imposition of the all-red era, First's London buses included yellow and white relief in the red livery.

The Brighton & Hove company was another early customer for the Trident, buying 20 East Lancs Lolyne-bodied 78-seat examples in 1999. What was, numerically, the first one is seen here when new at Brighton's Old Steine.

Above: Metroline bought Tridents with 9.9m (32ft 5in)-long 63-seat Alexander ALX400 bodies for its London operation in 1999, like this one approaching Kilburn, followed by an example of another popular Dennis model, the Dart SLF with Plaxton Pointer body.

Right: The Nottingham City Transport livery seems to accentuate the depth of the side windows of this early 88-seat East Lancs Lolyne-bodied Trident, one of 12 of its kind, photographed when new in 1999. (Robert McGillivray)

Lothian Region Transport adopted this harlequin livery to distinguish its low-floor buses. This Trident, new in 1999, with Plaxton President dual-door 75-seat body, is in Currie with low-key route branding below the upper deck windows.

The Oxford Bus Company bought 20 Alexander ALX400-bodied 71-seat two-door Tridents in 1999 for its growing network of park & ride services. This one is at the Pear Tree Park & Ride site in 2006.

The long-established Manchester-area independent operator, Mayne, bought this 81-seat East Lancs Lolyne-bodied Trident in 1999, seen here in the High Street in 2005, which proclaimed to be the 'Easy Access Bus'. (Mark Lyons)

Alexander ALX400-bodied Tridents quickly appeared in Stagecoach fleets outside London. This 1999 10.5m (34ft 5in) 80-seat Stagecoach Manchester example, dubbed 'LoLiner', emerges from the murk of the roadway below the Exchange Square shopping centre in 2002.

When it was in local authority ownership, Preston Bus bought 17 Tridents with East Lancs bodies, like this 85-seat 2000 delivery in Preston bus station in 2005. Like many of the early customers for low-floor buses, Preston Bus reminded potential passengers that this was an Easy Access Bus – though rather more subtly than many other companies. (Mark Lyons)

Above: Arriva The Shires bought Alexander ALX400-bodied 78-seat Tridents in 2000 for its lengthy interurban 500 route linking Aylesbury and Watford; however, by 2012, it was operating in Oxfordshire, seen here leaving Oxford railway station.

Left: Leon of Finningley was one of the independent operators that famously ran routes into Doncaster. This 2000-delivered Trident with East Lancs Lolyne 81-seat body was photographed in Finningley in 2002. (Roger Hall)

Another of the Manchester area independent operators, R Bullock of Cheadle, was an early customer for low-floor double-deckers. This 2000 East Lancs Lolyne-bodied 82-seat Trident is in Manchester's Portland Street in 2007.

Above: Liveried for the 900 limited stop service linking central Birmingham with the airport, a 2003 Trident/Alexander 73-seat ALX400 picks up passengers at the airport in 2004. (Roger Hall)

Right: A 2005 First Devon & Cornwall 10.3m (33ft 8in) Trident/East Lancs Myllennium Lolyne 78-seater, colourfully liveried for the Tamar Link service, working in partnership with Plymouth Council and the Department for Transport, leaves the Torpoint Ferry at Devonport en route for Plymouth in 2005. (Mark Lyons)

The Stagecoach Group continued to specify ALX400 bodies on Trident chassis for its other UK fleets. This 2006 Stagecoach Strathtay 10.5m (34ft 5in) 75-seat example is crossing the River Tay in Perth in 2008.

Chapter 6

Volvo B7L and B7TL

Volvo started building cars at Gothenburg, Sweden, and, in 1927, built its first bus. From 1972, it exported the single-deck B58, and later the B10M mid-engined single-deck chassis, to the UK and quickly won a substantial chunk of the market. Its first UK double-deck chassis was the front-engined B55 Ailsa in 1973, followed in 1982 by the mid-engined B10MD/Citybus chassis. These sold in respectable numbers, but following Volvo's acquisition of Leyland Bus in 1988, it offered the rear-engined Volvo Olympian, the most successful of the last generation of step-entrance double-deckers.

After its false start with a 1997 prototype based on its B7L single-deck chassis, Volvo redesigned its low-floor double-deck chassis with a transverse engine to suit UK preferences. Two models were introduced in 1999 – the B7L and B7TL. The B7 was similar to the 1997 bus and sold to operators of open-top tours, and in three-axle form to First Glasgow. The B7TL with transverse engine was by far the most popular choice, and Volvo quickly made up for lost time with substantial orders from all sectors of the UK bus market. The B7TL has been bodied by Alexander, East Lancs, Plaxton and Wright.

Lothian Buses majored on Dennis Tridents in the early years of low-floor double-deckers but also bought a small batch of Volvo B7TL with 75-seat Plaxton President bodies, seen here in the centre of Edinburgh when new in 2000.

Showing only the Transdev fleet name, a London United 2000-delivered B7TL with 63-seat Plaxton President body is pictured in Kingston in 2010. The lower deck window arrangement highlights the centrally situated staircase, which was a feature of earlier London low-floor double-deckers.

An early B7TL customer, Solent Blue Line, based in Eastleigh, was originally linked to the Southern Vectis company and is now part of the Go South Coast operation. This is a 2001 B7TL with an East Lancs Myllennium Vyking 73-seat body, seen in Southampton in 2004. (Mark Lyons)

Above: Step-entrance and low-floor Whippet double-deckers side by side in Huntingdon bus station in 2005. The Alexander-bodied Volvo B10M Citybus on the left was new in 1988, contrasting with the 2001 B7TL with an East Lancs Vyking 75-seat body on the right. The B10M had an underfloor engine, which raised the entrance and lower deck floor considerably – note the two-level entrance step. Whippet Coaches, based in Swavesey, Cambridgeshire, has existed for more than a century. (Roger Hall)

Left: Reliance of Sutton-on-the-Forest, operating between York and Easingwold, was an early independent customer for the B7TL/Wright Eclipse Gemini combination. This 2002 delivery is in Easingwold.

Pictured at Hyde Park Corner in 2003, a First London 2002 B7TL/Plaxton President 65-seater in First's version of the mainly red London livery with yellow and white relief.

Above: Go-Ahead London General bought 52 of these 10.4m (34ft 1in) B7TLs with East Lancs Myllennium Vyking 68-seat bodies in 2002. This one is picking up passengers at Wimbledon Station in 2007.

Right: East Thames Buses was set up by London Buses in 2000 to operate tendered routes that had been operated by Harris Bus. Crossing Waterloo Bridge in 2015 is a 2002 B7TL with 75-seat Wright bodywork. In 2009, the East Thames operation passed to Go-Ahead.

In 2003, First Glasgow bought ten of these B7TLT three-axle chassis with East Lancs Nordic 95-seat bodies, as seen here in Clydebank in 2006. Similar buses, but with left-hand drive, had been delivered in 2001 to local operators for service in Copenhagen.

Above: Crossing Piccadilly Circus when new in 2003, a London General B7TL/Wright with a 10.1m (33ft 1in) 64-seat Wright body.

Left: Although London buses are worked hard and tend to have shorter lives with their original owners, this Go-Ahead London Central 2003 B7TL with 64-seat Plaxton President body was still in service, here in Croydon, in 2016.

Strathtay Scottish, owned by the Barnsley-based Traction Group, received seven of these 76-seat East Lancs Vyking-bodied B7TLs in 2003; one is heading west along Dundee's Nethergate when new.

Above: Bournemouth Transport, trading as Yellow Buses, bought this B7TL with East Lancs Vyking 76-seat body in 2003, seen here in Christchurch when new.

Right: London United bought 45 B7TLs with East Lancs Myllennium Vyking 69-seat bodies in 2004. This one is in Kingston in 2015.

Turning into Camden High Street in 2012, a 2004 First London B7TL with a 10.1m (33ft 1in) Wright 59-seat body and an impressively long fleet number.

Above: A 2005 Go North East B7TL/Wright 74-seater branded for the X10 Newcastle–Middlesbrough service emerges from Newcastle's Eldon Square bus station in 2008.

Left: Before Wilts & Dorset adopted the 'more' branding, a 2005 B7TL with East Lancs Myllennium Vyking 78-seat body leaves The Square at Bournemouth in 2008, bound for Lymington. The slightly shallower upper deck windows reveal that it is a convertible open-topper, with the ability to run in open-top form after removal and storage of the rear part of the roof.

A Solent Blue Line, now trading as Bluestar, 2006 Volvo B7TL with ADL Enviro400 79-seat body, seen in 2007, which had started life as an ADL demonstrator; this was the only B7TL to receive an E400 body. (Mark Lyons)

Chapter 7

Scania N series

Scania built its first bus in Sweden in 1911 and had first ventured into the UK bus market in 1969 in collaboration with Metro-Cammell Weymann (MCW) to produce the Metro-Scania single-deck city bus, based on the existing Scania BR111 model. A second model developed with MCW was the Metropolitan double-decker, introduced in 1973.

Scania's return to the UK double-deck market was in 1980 with its step-entrance N112DRB and N113DRB chassis, and, in 2003, it introduced the low-floor N94UD, which, with 10.6m (34ft 8in) East Lancs bodywork, was marketed by Scania as the OmniDekka. In 2005, it launched the CN94UD OmniCity with Polish-built body.

More recently, Scania has developed its N2xxUD series of models, including gas-powered chassis, all with Alexander bodies.

Right: Metrobus, part of the Go-Ahead Group, bought Scania OmniDekkas for its services on the fringes of London. The OmniDekka was a collaboration between Scania and East Lancs, and this colourful 2003 10.6m (34ft 8in) 72-seater is in Bromley High Street in 2004. (Mark Lyons)

Below: Climbing inland from the Jurassic Coast near Abbotsbury in 2004, a new First Hampshire & Dorset N94UD OmniDekka with East Lancs 69-seat body, liveried for the lengthy X53 Jurassic Coast Coastlinx service between Poole and Exeter. (Mark Lyons)

Several London operators bought low-floor Scania double-deckers, including RATP Group's London United company. This N94UD OmniDekka with 10.6m (34ft 8in) East Lancs 71-seat body was new in 2005 and is pictured in Kingston in 2017.

First Scotland East invested in 24 N94UD/East Lancs 77-seat OmniDekkas in 2005, as seen here at Livingston Centre heading for Edinburgh when new.

Scania offered the OmniCity as a complete bus, built in Poland, and Lothian Buses was an early customer for the model, based on the N94UD chassis. This 2006 68-seat example is in Edinburgh's Princes Street, branded for the 100 Airlink service.

Operating on the lengthy Regency Route between Tunbridge Wells and Brighton, a 2007 10.6m (34ft 8in) N94UD/ East Lancs OmniDekka with 79-seat body is pictured in Brighton's Old Steine on the last leg of its journey in 2009. Since 1999, Brighton & Hove buses have carried the names of prominent deceased local people; Samuel Lewis was a money lender and benefactor.

Above: A Metroline 2007 N230UD with 10.8m (35ft 4in) East Lancs Olympus 68-seat dual-door body is pictured in New Oxford Street, London in 2012.

Left: Cardiff Bus bought 13 of these N270UDs with East Lancs Olympus 74-seat bodies in 2007. This one is in St Mary Street in 2010.

A 2008 N230UD with 80-seat East Lancs Olympus body running for Burton's Coaches, trading as Network Colchester. It is seen here in Greenstead having been recently delivered. (Russell Young)

Above: The principal Isle of Wight bus company, Southern Vectis, part of the Go-Ahead Group, operated this 76-seat 2008 all-Scania OmniCity on N230UD chassis, seen here at Ryde Esplanade when new. (Mark Lyons)

Right: Johnsons of Henley-in-Arden operated this Scania N230UD with Optare Olympus 80-seat bodywork, pictured when new in Stratford upon Avon on the Excelbus X20, linking Birmingham with Stratford. (Mark Lyons)

RATP Group's London United company was a major customer for the Polish-built OmniCity, taking more than 200 between 2006 and 2010. This 2009 63-seat dual-door N230UD is at Kingston's Cromwell Road bus station in 2017, wearing the 'heritage' livery as used by London United before the all-red rule was imposed.

An Oxford Bus 2010 N230UD with 80-seat ADL E400 body leaves Oxford railway station in 2012, bound for Blackbird Leys.

Nottingham City Transport, the largest of the surviving municipal operators in England, has been a faithful Scania customer. This 2013 N230UD with 74-seat ADL E400 bodywork, is in Nottingham, liveried for the frequent 43 Red Line service. (Mark Lyons)

Hackney Community Transport, which trades in London as CT Plus, operates the Metrobus M1 service in Bristol under contract to First West of England, using ADL E400City-bodied 70-seat CNG-powered N280UDs, as seen here in Broad Quay, Bristol. This is one of 21 bought in 2018. (Mark Lyons)

First Eastern Counties bought 19 N280UDs with 65-seat ADL E400City bodies in 2020. This newly delivered example, in Excel livery for the Norwich–Peterborough service, is in Peterborough. (Russell Young)

A First Essex 2020 N280UD with ADL E400 63-seat body at Stansted Airport is seen working on the Essex Airlink service to Chelmsford when new. (Russell Young)

Delivered in mid-2021 to the Stagecoach West fleet, this N250UD with ADL 71-seat E400 body is on The Promenade in Cheltenham, in the amber yellow livery introduced in 2020 to denote vehicles on longer-distance services. (Mark Lyons)

Chapter 8

Alexander Dennis Enviro400

The Scottish coachbuilder, Alexander, began as a family firm that started building bodies for the buses it operated in 1924 and grew to supply the expanding SMT Group of companies. When the Group was taken into state control in 1949, the Alexander family retained the coachbuilding business, which meant that its bodies were available to a much wider range of customers.

The Alexander business changed hands in the 1990s and was in danger of closure following the collapse of the Mayflower Group, but with Scottish investment it combined with chassis builder Dennis to create ADL.

ADL introduced the Enviro400 (E400) in 2005 to replace the highly successful ALX400 range. This used a modified Trident chassis, built at Guildford, and a restyled Alexander body, built at Falkirk. Although this was presented and marketed as a complete vehicle, the E40D chassis was also specified with East Lancs and Optare bodies.

The original styling was replaced by the MMC version in 2014 and a City version, initially aimed at London fleets, which took some styling cues from the Wright bus, New Routemaster.

Although designed as a diesel-engined model, environmental concerns led to the introduction of new technologies, and the Enviro400 spawned hybrid, smart hybrid, full electric, electric range, biogas and, most recently, hydrogen fuel cell versions. The full electric has a chassis developed by BYD (Build Your Dreams) in China, and the biogas version is on a Scania chassis.

The Alexander E400 was mainly built as an integral vehicle, combining Alexander bodywork on a Dennis chassis. Stagecoach East London was an obvious customer for the model, which had more rounded lines than its ALX400 predecessor. This 2006 10.8m (35ft 4in) bus, No 18500, was the first production E400, and it was the replacement for the Stagecoach bus destroyed in Tavistock Square in the terrorist attacks of 7 July 2005; it was named *Spirit of London* as a tribute to the victims of these attacks. It is at Upper Street in 2007. (Mark Lyons)

Fresh out of the box at Vauxhall bus station in London, with the distinctive outlines of the St George's Wharf apartments behind, a London General E400 with 10.1m (33ft 1in) 67-seat body is seen in 2006.

Yellow Buses, by this time part of the Transdev group, bought this 78-seat E400 in 2007, seen here at The Square in Bournemouth in 2008. It had been a former ADL demonstrator.

Stagecoach bought E400s for its Cambridge Park & Ride services – this 10.8m (35ft 4in)-long 81-seater, new in 2007, crosses the River Cam in 2008.

Quality Line, part of the Epsom Coaches group, bought ten dual-door 10.1m (33ft 1in) 67-seat E400s in 2007 to operate on two routes into Kingston, under contract to Transport for London. This one is in Kingston in 2010.

Above: Leaving Newcastle's Haymarket bus station in 2008 for Blyth is a 2007 Arriva North East E400 80-seater.

Left: London General's Optare-bodied Tridents were unique in London service; it bought 54 of these 10.3m (33ft 8in)-long Optare Olympus-bodied dual-door 64-seat examples in 2008–09, and two are seen here laying over at Kingston's Fairfield bus station in 2009.

Western Greyhound, based in Summercourt, near Newquay, provided local services in Devon and Cornwall until 2015. In 2009, it bought two of these 78-seat E400s for the 510 Exeter–Newquay service, one of which is seen here at Okehampton in 2010. These were the only double-deckers the company bought new. (Mark Lyons)

Above: A Scottish Stagecoach E400, a 2009 81-seat example, at Anstruther in 2016 on the Coastliner 95 route, linking Leven with St Andrews.

Right: Three-axle double-deckers are still rare in urban service in the UK, but First Glasgow bought 25 of these 82-seat Enviro500s in 2009. One is seen here turning into Glasgow's Argyle Street when new.

Newport Bus, one of the two remaining local authority bus fleets in Wales, bought five of these 76-seat E400s in 2012. This one is seen in Custom House Street, Cardiff, bound for its hometown in 2018. (Russell Young)

Solent Blue Line provides the Unilink service for the University of Southampton. This is a 2013 dual-door 65-seat E400 in 2014. (Mark Lyons)

The Stagecoach Manchester fleet was an early user of the updated Enviro400 MMC body style, seen here on a 2014 10.9m (35ft 8in)-metre 80-seater in the Piccadilly Gardens bus station in 2015.

A 2014 E400 delivery to First South Yorkshire at Sheffield railway station in 2017, a 75-seater, one of 15 allocated to Sheffield.

A 2014 Reading Buses 11.5m (37ft 7in)-long 76-seat E400MMC, liveried for the Emerald group of routes, negotiates the bridge over the River Kennet at Duke Street in central Reading in 2018. The MMC represented an upgrading of the E400 design.

Cardiff Bus bought ten 75-seat E400MMCs in 2015, as seen here in 2018, with the walls of Cardiff Castle in the background on the left.

A 2015 delivery to Go-Ahead East Anglia's Konectbus fleet, a coach-seated 76-seat E400 is operating the Straight 8 service from Norwich to Dereham, where it was photographed in the High Street in 2020, heading for Toftwood. (Mark Lyons)

Universitybus of Hatfield was set up by the University of Hertfordshire in 1992 and now trades as Uno. It has invested in E400City models for its Comet service linking Hatfield and Barnet, with London Underground stations at Edgware and Queensbury. This newly introduced 10.5m (34ft 5in)-long 74-seat version is at Hatfield. (Mark Lyons)

Al's Coaches of Birkenhead, trading as Happy Al's, bought this 86-seat E400MMC in 2017. It is in Chester, en route for West Kirkby, in 2021. (Russell Young)

A 2018 E400City, delivered to Southern Transit of Upper Beeding in Shoreham when new, subtly displaying the Citymaster name above the front wheel. (Mark Lyons)

Arriva's Sapphire identity is used for upmarket services like the 166 between Castleford and Leeds, where this 2017 delivery, with 63 coach seats, is seen in 2018.

A First Leeds E400MMC in Skipton High Street in 2018 – a 74-seat 2017 delivery, branded for the X84 Wharfedale Connection linking Leeds with Otley, Ilkley and Skipton.

A Stagecoach 2018 10.9m (35ft 8in)-long E400MMC with 80 seats, branded for the Pronto service linking Chesterfield, Mansfield and Nottingham; it is in Mansfield Road, Nottingham in 2018. (Mark Lyons)

The latest FirstBus livery style enables buses to be colour-coded for easy recognition by passengers. A newly delivered 2019 First Glasgow 74-seat E400MMC, liveried for First Glasgow's 38 route, passes the former Glasgow Stock Exchange building in Nelson Mandela Square.

Borders Buses, part of the West Coast Motors group, replaced many former First routes in the Scottish Borders, and, in 2019, bought three of these E400MMC 78-seaters, seen here in Galashiels in 2020. (Richard Walter)

Go North East bought three of these E400MMCs in 2019, liveried for the X Lines group of express routes linking Newcastle with Consett, Stanley and Sunnyside. This one is in Newcastle in 2021. (Richard Walter)

Following Go-Ahead's acquisition of the East Yorkshire company in 2018, a new livery style was introduced, as worn by this 2020-delivered E400MMC, one of a batch of eight, in York in 2021; it is branded for the Bridlington–York EastRider service. (Richard Walter)

CityZap is the brand name for Transdev's York–Leeds service, and this 2020 E400City 68-seater is in York in 2021. (Richard Walter)

Chapter 9

Volvo B9TL

In 2006, Volvo replaced its popular B7TL chassis with the B9TL, meeting EuroIV and then EuroV emission standards. Over the next eight years, B9TLs entered service throughout the British Isles with bodies by Alexander, East Lancs/Optare and MCV, with the greatest number carrying Wrightbus Gemini 2 bodies.

In 2013, the B9TL was succeeded by the B5TL, a lighter chassis meeting EuroVI requirements. The B5TL was mainly bodied by Wright, but some were also bodied by ADL.

Sanders Coaches, based in Holt in Norfolk, bought this B9TL with 82-seat East Lancs Olympus body in 2008, seen here highlighting its clean air credentials in Castle Meadow, Norwich, in 2009. (Mark Lyons)

First's Aberdeen fleet included deliveries of Wright-bodied B9TLs, like this 2008 74-seat example, branded for the upmarket 19 Platinum service, against the impressive backdrop of the 19th century granite-built Marischal College in 2014.

A rare combination, seen in Kingston in 2009 – a Go-Ahead London General B9TL with Alexander Dennis Enviro400 10.35m (34ft) 65-seat body, new in 2008.

A 2008 Arriva Derby B9TL/Wright in Derby in 2009 with subtle branding for the frequent 44/45 service. The Wright Eclipse Gemini body had seats for 70 passengers.

A 2009 East Yorkshire B9TL/Wright 74-seater, in the centre of Hull in 2011. At the time, East Yorkshire was the largest family-owned bus company in the UK, and, in 2018, it was acquired by the Go-Ahead Group.

East London Transit (ELT) is an attempt to design a bus service that makes maximum use of busways and sections of reserved road, to give passengers a speedier journey where there are currently no rail services. The first buses to serve ELT were 10.4m (34ft 1in) Go-Ahead B9TLs, new in 2010 with Wright 56-seat bodies, as seen at Thames View Health Centre, Barking, in 2010. It is possible this busway could be upgraded to a tramway in the future.

VM1, in Go-Ahead London's Docklands Buses fleet, was a 2011 Volvo B9TL with Egyptian-built MCV 63-seat body, here in North Woolwich when new. Go-Ahead went on to buy further examples, but on Volvo B5LH chassis, in 2016–17. (Mark Lyons)

A Brighton & Hove 2011 B9TL with 71-seat Wright body carries branding for the 6 route as it heads into the centre of Brighton in 2013.

Above: In addition to its open-top tours operation, Bath Bus Company, part of the French-owned RATP Group, also operated this service linking Bath and Bristol Airport. This is a 2012 B9TL with MCV 63-seat body, seen in 2015. (Mark Lyons)

Right: A 2012 Metroline B9TL with 62-seat Wright Eclipse Gemini 2 body passes an Arriva London Volvo hybrid at Mornington Crescent in 2013.

In Skipton, in 2017, on the Transdev Burnley & Pendle's Witchway service to Manchester, is a 2013 B9TL/Wright with 67 coach seats.

Chapter 10
Other Diesel Models

MAN and BCI

The long-established German truck and bus builder MAN enjoyed some success in the UK with its 18.220 and 18.240 single-deck low-floor models in the Stagecoach fleet. In 2006, it launched its fully low-floor ND243 double-deck model into the UK. The prototype, and only, UK version received a low-height 4m (13ft 1in) double-deck East Lancs body; it was initially trialled with Reading Buses.

The Australian firm BCI builds buses in China, and the Purfleet-based bus operator and dealer Ensignbus placed three 12.5m (41ft) BCI Enterprise double-deckers in service in 2016, followed by 12 10.8m (35ft 4in) CitiRider models in 2017 and two more Enterprises in 2019.

MAN dipped a toe in the UK double-deck market with its fully low-floor ND243 model, first seen at a bus show in 2006. The prototype, here working for Reading Buses in 2007, had a 4m (13ft 1in)-high East Lancs Kinetic+ 79-seat body; it remains the only example bought for UK use.

Reading Buses has always been prepared to consider new types of bus for its fleet, and it borrowed this triaxle 98-seat BCI Enterprise from Ensignbus of Purfleet in 2016. (Mark Lyons)

Optare, which had previously built double-deck bodies on DAF chassis, concentrated for many years on building innovative single-deck models but turned to building complete double-deckers with the Metrodecker model in 2016. This pre-production MD1050, 10.5m (34ft 5in) long with 63 seats and dual doors, is at North Greenwich when new with London Central. (Mark Lyons)

Another pre-production Optare Metrodecker was trialled by various bus companies, including Go North East. This 2016 MD1114 11.1m (36ft 4in)-long 83-seater is leaving Newcastle's Eldon Square bus station in 2017.

London General evaluated this 2018 BCI Enterprise dual-door triaxle 78-seater, seen here in Westminster Bridge Road in 2019. (Mark Lyons)

Chapter 11

Wright Early Hybrids and NBfL

W right had firmly established its role as a major mainstream builder of double-deck bodies on DAF/VDL and Volvo chassis, and, with the 2DL model, had created a complete double-decker. When initial interest had been shown in diesel-electric hybrid double-deckers, it built 14 Gemini 2HEVs 'seed' vehicles, mainly for London operators in 2007–08.

Following a design competition, the Wright New Bus for London (NBfL), or New Routemaster, was supplied to TfL between 2012 and 2018 and leased to London operators on a route-by-route basis. The hybrid 11.3m (37ft 1in)-long bus has three entrances and 62 seats, and 999 examples were built. The 1,000th bus was a shorter variant, 10.2m (33ft 5in) long with 54 seats.

Wright built early hybrid buses for First London. This Gemini 2 65-seat hybrid, one of five delivered in 2008, lays over in Golders Green bus station in 2009.

A very early London hybrid double-decker, a 2008 Go-Ahead Pulsar Gemini hybrid 10.4m (34ft 1in)-long 65-seater, is seen at Trafalgar Square in 2009.

Wright's NBfL – or New Routemaster, or even Borismaster – first appeared in service in 2012, and 1,000 examples were built between 2012 and 2018. All but one were 11.3m (37ft 1in)-long 62-seat triple-door buses. Some of the early NBfL deliveries carried London registration marks, but these were quickly changed to the LTZ marks. At Hampstead Heath terminus, in 2013, are two examples operated by Metroline: LT11 with its LK13 FJJ registration (later LTZ 1013) and LT39 with LTZ 1039.

A 2013 London United-operated NBfL heads along Piccadilly in 2014.

An expensive bus queue in John Prince's Street, just west of Oxford Circus, early in 2017. Six NBfLs, collectively worth well over £1m, gather for reasons lost in the mists of time. In front are three Arriva-operated examples – LT341, at the front, was new in 2014.

In 2014, when London's NBfL fleet was still allowed to run with open rear platforms, 'old' Routemaster-style, a newly delivered London United example is seen at Marble Arch.

Chapter 12

Alexander Dennis E400H

A s concerns increased about the effect of vehicle emissions on climate change, there was pressure on bus builders to develop greener models. Transport for London was keen to see greener buses on its routes, and ADL, Volvo and Wright developed diesel-electric hybrid models. The ADL offering, the Enviro400H (E400H), first appeared in 2008 and has sold in substantial numbers to fleets in London and around the UK.

Metroline was one of the London operators to take early deliveries of ADL hybrids. In Kilburn High Road in 2009, a 2008 10.1m (33ft 1in) 63-seat E400H delivery.

Another of London's first ADL hybrids, a 10.1m (33ft 1in) London General 63-seat E400H; it was delivered in 2009 and declared itself to be 'Another red bus going green for London'. It was photographed at Victoria in 2012.

Operators of early hybrid double-deckers made sure prospective passengers knew what they would be travelling on. This Thames Electric Hybrid, a 76-seat 2010 E400H, owned by Thames Travel of Wallingford, is in Arborfield when new. In 2011, Thames Travel passed into the Go-Ahead group, under Oxford Bus. (Mark Lyons)

In 2011, Oxford Bus bought E400Hs for its Park & Ride services; this 10.9m (35ft 8in) 77-seater is seen crossing the Magdalen Bridge over the River Cherwell in 2013.

National Express' Scottish outpost at Dundee received nine of these ADL E400H 78-seaters in 2013, branded for the high-frequency 5 route; this one is seen on its first day in service.

Reading Buses bought batches of ADL hybrids. This one in Friar Street, Reading, in 2016, and new in 2011, is an 11.4m (37ft 4in) 76-seater, and it wears a distinctive, purple-based livery that featured on successive generations of the buses for the 17 route. This bus, with others, has subsequently been converted to run as a pure diesel.

Lothian Buses bought a batch of 15 E400H 77-seat models in 2011, clad in a madder/gold version of the fleet livery. This one is in Edinburgh's Princes Street when new. Like early hybrids elsewhere in the UK, these have been converted to run as normal diesels.

East Yorkshire bought ten 77-seat E400H models in 2011 in fleet livery but drawing attention to their green credentials, telling passers-by that these buses are saving 240 tonnes of CO2 every year. It is in Hull in 2011.

Three E400H VE types were delivered to Tower Transit in London in 2015. These 64-seaters were Virtual Electrics, able to run mainly in electric mode with under-bus chargers at the Walthamstow terminus of the 69 route. This recharging facility has since been discontinued. One turns into Walthamstow bus station in 2016.

A 2015 E400H delivery to National Express West Midlands, wearing a special green livery for the 1 route. A 77-seater, it is leaving Dudley bus station in 2013.

The ADL E400City model took some design cues from the NBfL design. This recently received CTPlus 10.4m (34ft 1in) 66-seater is one of 49 delivered in 2015–19 and is in Threadneedle Street in 2016, with the Bank of England on its right.

A 2018 66-seat 10.4m (34ft 1in)-long E400H delivered to Abellio London passes St Pancras International station in 2019, at the start of its journey to Clapham Park.

A new E400H 79-seater is wearing the latest version of Stagecoach's local service livery at Aberdeen in 2021. (Keith McGillivray)

Chapter 13

Volvo B5LH

Volvo, with a substantial presence in the London bus market, developed the B5LH diesel-electric hybrid model, which was introduced in 2009. Most have carried Wright, and, more recently, MCV bodies, and a smaller number have been built with Alexander bodies.

Right: On test in Green Lanes in Haringey in 2009, one of Arriva's first hybrid double-deckers; it would shortly carry fleet number HV2. It is a 60-seat 10.4m (34ft 1in) Volvo B5LH/Wright.

Below: The Greater Manchester-area independent, Bullocks of Cheadle, bought four of these early B5LH with Wright 73-seat bodies in 2011. Although the company name is not displayed, the registration mark helps identification in London Road, Manchester in 2015, as it passes a sister vehicle.

Above: A 2011 First Leeds B5LH with Wright 64-seat body in City Square, Leeds, wearing the silver livery style that was initially used to promote the hybrid buses in the First fleet.

Left: An early Go-Ahead London Central B5LH/Wright 10.4m (34ft 1in) 60-seater, new in 2011, leaves Whitehall in 2012, with a subtle reference to its green credentials on its rear flanks.

In First's silver livery carried by its early hybrid deliveries, a First Manchester 2011 B5LH with 64-seat Wright Gemini 2 body in Manchester's Piccadilly in 2013.

Above: Oxford Bus bought B5LHs with a lower-height version of the familiar Wright Eclipse Gemini 2 body, like this 2012 72-seat example approaching Oxford Station in 2013.

Right: The Australian-owned company Tower Transit acquired much of First's London operations in 2013. This B5LH with 10.6m (34ft 8in) 62-seat Wright Gemini 3 body leaves Golders Green's busy bus station, having been newly delivered in 2016.

A 2013 National Express West Midlands B5LH/Wright Gemini 2 65-seater is seen when new at Dudley bus station, branded for the 1 route and displaying its green credentials.

A London United 2015 62-seat 10.5m (34ft 5in) B5LH with Wright Gemini 3 bodywork passes under the railway as it enters central Kingston in 2019.

An unusual combination – Stagecoach London bought 42 of these 10.5m (34ft 5in) B5LHs with ADL Enviro400MMC 63-seat bodies in 2015; this one is seen in Greenwich when new.

A Metroline 2015 62-seat 10.5m (34ft 5in) Volvo B5LH with the original style of Wright Gemini 3 bodywork, distinguished by its shallower upper-deck windows, crosses into The Strand in London in 2017.

Lothian Buses bought 20 of these Volvo B5LHs with 74-seat Wright Gemini 3 bodies in 2015. This one is seen in Ocean Terminal, Edinburgh, when new.

Above: Arriva North West & Wales received 40 of these low-height Wright Gemini 3-bodied B5LHs in 2017. This one, proclaiming its green credentials, is seen in Liverpool. (Russell Young)

Left: London United has bought Wright Gemini 3 bodies on B5LH chassis for the services it operates for Kingston University. This 11.4m (37ft 4in) 77-seater, complete with glazed staircase panels, is in Kingston when new in 2017.

Go-Ahead's London companies turned to MCV for the bodywork on its B5LHs from 2016. This 2016 example, with 10.5m (34ft 5in) 62-seat MCV eVoSeti body, is in Wimbledon in 2017.

Chapter 14

Wright Gemini 2DL

Continuing the relationship between Wrightbus and VDL (Van de Leegte), the integral 10.4m (34ft 1in)-long 2DL was developed for the UK market, combining a lighter-weight Gemini 2 body and a VDL DB300 chassis module. It was introduced in 2009, and Arriva, which had been the main customer for the DAF/VDL DB250LF model, was by far the main customer for the Gemini 2DL.

Wright and VDL combined to produce the Wright Gemini 2DL, essentially an Eclipse Gemini 2 body on a VDL DB300 underframe. The majority were built for Arriva's London fleet, and this 2013 10.4m (34ft 1in) 65-seat example is crossing Waterloo Bridge in 2017.

An Arriva London 2011 Gemini 2DL 65-seater in Camden Road in 2012.

A 2013 Arriva Gemini 65-seat 2DL model passes the 1920s art deco mass of the former Carreras cigarette factory, known as the Black Cat Factory, in Hampstead Road in 2013.

Chapter 15

Volvo B5TL and B8L

Volvo replaced its popular B9TL model with the B5TL in 2014, and while previous diesel Volvos had been popular with London operators, they were turning to hybrids at the time, and so the B5TL sold particularly well in Ireland and with Lothian Buses. The great majority have Wright bodies, but there have also been MCV bodies, and Lothian's most recent deliveries have Alexander bodies.

The three-axle Volvo B8L diesel double-deck chassis was designed mainly for overseas markets, but, in 2019, Lothian Buses took delivery of 63 with 100-seat ADL Enviro400XLB bodies, and followed this with a batch of 15 81-seaters for its Airlink service. Stagecoach bought 12 98-seaters in 2019 to use on the Cambridgeshire Guided Busway. Golden Tours of London has taken eight with MCV eVoSeti 80-seat bodies.

This 2014 B5TL/Wright 63-seater in Go-Ahead's Metrobus fleet in Croydon in 2016 started life as a Volvo demonstrator. The B5TL was less common in London service than its B7TL and B9TL predecessors, as most orders started to move away from diesel buses like the B5TL to diesel-electric hybrids like Volvo's B5LH.

Volvo provided 'seed' vehicles of new models to prospective customers. This 2014 B5TL with Wright Eclipse Gemini 3 73-seat body was loaned to Lothian Buses when new and featured an early version of the glazed staircase panels would become more familiar. It is at the Mound, Edinburgh, in 2014.

Transdev has invested in B5TLs with Wright 63-seat bodies for its Coastliner network linking Leeds and York with the Yorkshire coast. A 2016 delivery is in York in 2021. (Richard Walter)

Translink in Northern Ireland bought B5TLs with 69-seat Wright bodies for the Metro network in Belfast. This 2017 example is in Donegall Square in 2020. (Mark Lyons)

Right: Lothian Buses has favoured high-capacity double-deckers and in 2019 bought 63 of these 100-seat triaxle Volvo B8Ls with Alexander Dennis 400XLB bodies. This one is in Bruntsfield, Edinburgh, in 2019.

Below: For its routes on the Busway, the 16-mile Cambridgeshire Guided Busway, Stagecoach bought 12 of these B8Ls with ADL Enviro400XLB 98-seat bodies in 2019 – similar to the buses built for Lothian Buses earlier that year. The ocean green livery is used to denote specialist services. (Russell Young)

Chapter 16

Wright StreetDeck

Wright moved increasingly towards building complete double-deckers, following its experience with the 2DL and NBfL examples. The integral StreetDeck was introduced in 2015 and has proved popular with First and Go-Ahead fleets in Britain, and with Citybus and Ulsterbus in Northern Ireland.

Left: Reading Buses took delivery of a batch of six 70-seat Wright StreetDecks in 2016, as seen here in central Reading in Orange Routes livery in 2017.

Below: Supplied to First Eastern Counties in 2016, this is a 73-seat StreetDeck, seen in the Norwich Pink Line livery variant when new. (Russell Young)

First Leicester has been another recipient of StreetDeck 73-seaters; this 2016 example, in Charles Street in 2020, is branded for the frequent 54 route. (Russell Young)

First's latest livery scheme allows local names and distinctive colours to be applied to its fleet. In Leeds City Square in 2018 is a 73-seat 2017 First Leeds StreetDeck.

Go North East bought 19 of these 10.6m (34ft 8in)-long 68-seat StreetDecks in 2017, as seen here in The Angel livery in 2020, as it passes under a GB Railfreight Class 66 in Newcastle. (Russell Young)

An Oxford Bus lower-height StreetDeck 82-seater, new in 2018, in St Aldates, Oxford in 2019 in BrookesBus livery.

Between 2018 and 2021, Translink in Northern Ireland placed more than 100 StreetDecks in service with its Citybus and Ulsterbus fleets. This 2018 71-seater is in Ulsterbus Urby livery at Millisle in 2020. (Mark Lyons)

Diamond North West, part of the Rotala empire and operating in Greater Manchester, bought large quantities of these 10.5m (34ft 5in)-long 74-seat StreetDecks in 2019. This one is Manchester-bound at Irlams o' th' Height when new. (Russell Young)

Preston Bus, part of the Rotala Group, has bought StreetDecks like this 2021 74-seat 10.5m (34ft 5in)-long example, seen leaving Preston's iconic bus station when new; it is branded for the 23 route and highlighting the 99-year history of this route. (Russell Young)

Go North East took delivery of 22 10.6m (34ft 8in) StreetDecks in 2020 in various versions of the X Lines livery, as seen here in Newcastle in 2021. (Richard Walter)

Chapter 17

Electric and Hydrogen Double-Deckers

W ith pressure on manufacturers to produce greener buses, there have been moves to design more environmentally friendly diesels, diesel-electric hybrids, CNG and biogas buses, and more recently battery electric and hydrogen buses. Single-deck electric buses have been around for some time, often hampered by the size and weight of the batteries, but technology has advanced to produce lighter and more practical electric buses, first single-deckers and, more recently, double-deckers. The double-deckers have been built by the Chinese firm BYD, also providing chassis for Alexander bodies.

More recently, there have been hydrogen double-deckers, first from Wrightbus and in development with ADL.

There have been many experimental battery-electric single-deckers over the years, and London fleets have been investing in the latest generation models. Electric double-deckers are a more recent development, and this is a 10.2m (33ft 5in)-long BYD K8SR 54-seater, one of five delivered to Metroline in 2016, seen here in Oxford Street in 2017.

A batch of 34 BYD D8UR/ ADL 70-seat electric double-deckers was supplied to Stagecoach companies in 2019. Most went to Manchester, but two, including this one, went to Cambridge, where it is on Park & Ride duties in 2020. (Russell Young)

Above: Two of the 32 BYD D8UR/ADL electric 70-seaters supplied to Stagecoach Manchester in Oxford Road in 2019, painted in the ocean green livery that denotes specialist vehicles. (Russell Young)

Right: Metroline was the first customer for Optare's Metrodecker, taking 31 MD1050EV 63-seaters in 2019–20, such as the one seen here at Kentish Town in 2020.

First York took delivery of 21 Optare Metrodecker MD1114EV dual-door 78-seaters in 2020; this newly delivered example in Station Road in York is in Park & Ride livery. (Russell Young)

Above: National Express Coventry received 29 of these BYD D8UR/ADL electrics in 2020. They are 65-seaters, and this newly delivered one is in Warwick Road, Coventry. (Russell Young)

Left: In 2020–21, Go-Ahead London invested heavily in these BYD D8URs with ADL Enviro400 City 67-seat dual-door bodies. This one is at Chingford Hatch in 2020. (Russell Young)

Go-Ahead London also bought seven Optare Metrodecker MD1050EV 63-seaters in 2021; this one is at Raynes Park in 2021. (Mark Lyons)

Above: In 2021, Lothian Buses placed in service four BYD D8UR/ADL electric 72-seaters funded by SP Energy Networks. This newly delivered example is in Edinburgh's Princes Street when new.

Right: The very first hydrogen double-deckers to enter service in the UK were 14 of these 65-seat Wrightbus StreetDecks for First Aberdeen in 2021, seen here when new. The Wrightbus hydrogen double-deck model has been given the StreetDeck Hydroliner name. The electric version is to be the StreetDeck Electroliner and the EuroVI diesel version, the StreetDeck Ultroliner. (Keith McGillivray)

The first hydrogen-powered double-deckers for London service were delivered to Metroline in 2021 – 20 Wright StreetDecks. This dual-door 61-seater is in East Acton when new. (Mark Lyons)

Chapter 18

Exports

U K chassis and body builders have, for decades, supplied double-deckers for customers around the world. For a time, Hong Kong and Singapore were the principal markets, but there were pockets of UK-built double-deckers in Europe, North and South America, the Middle East, Australia and, of course, Ireland.

When low-floor double-deckers came along, the greatest demand came from the Far East, but there has been a surge of interest in double-deckers as crowd-movers, and UK builders have won valuable business from often unexpected sources.

These could fill a book of their own, but as a tailpiece to this coverage of low-floor types for the UK market, here are a few examples of recent – one not so recent – deliveries that underline the importance of export markets to UK-based suppliers.

An order from an unexpected source came from Denmark, where City Trafik took 22 of these Volvo B7LTs with 76-seat Blackburn-built East Lancs three-door Nordic bodies in 2001 to operate for HT, the Copenhagen operator. One is seen here at Copenhagen Airport when new; Arriva Danmark took 14 similar buses in the same year. Ten similar buses, but with right-hand drive, 95 seats and single-door, were built for First Glasgow the following year.

Alexander became heavily involved in bodying double-deckers for export customers in the 1970s, and subsequently, as part of ADL, has also been engaged in building complete double-deckers for overseas markets. This Enviro500 is one of 19 three-door 80-seaters supplied in 2017–19 to PostAuto for use in Eastern Switzerland, and is seen in St Gallen in 2017. A further 13 were supplied to another operator for services around Lausanne in 2019. (Keith McGillivray)

BVG, the Berlin municipal operator, has ordered 200 ADL Enviro500 13.8m (45ft 3in)-long three-door 80-seaters, and the first two were supplied in 2020 with the balance of the order due in 2022. (Alexander Dennis)

Wright also became a major supplier of double-deck bodies for export customers. This is a 2019 Volvo B8L 90-seater for Kowloon Motor Bus, based in Hong Kong, seen in Kowloon when new. (Phil Halewood)

This 81-seat ADL Enviro500 SuperLo, seen when new in 2017 in downtown Toronto, Canada, comes from large batches supplied to GoTransit between 2016 and 2019. (Keith McGillivray)